Simple Machines
PULLEYS AND GEARS

David Glover

© 1997, 2006 Heinemann Library
a division of Reed Elsevier Inc.
Chicago, Illinois

Customer Service 888-454-2279
Visit our website at www.heinemannraintree.com

Designed by Victoria Bevan and Q2A Creative
Illustrations by Barry Atkinson (pp. 8, 9, 11, 17) and Tony Kenyon (p. 7)
Printed in China by WKT Company Ltd.

10 09 08
10 9 8 7 6 5

New edition ISBN: 1-4034-8564-X (hardback)
             1-4034-8593-3 (paperback)
             978-1-4034-8564-9 (hardback)
             978-1-4034-8593-9 (paperback)

The Library of Congress has cataloged the first edition as follows:
Glover, David, 1953 Sept. 4-
      Pulleys and gears / David Glover.
        p. cm. -- (Simple Machines)
      Includes index.
      Summary: Introduces the principles of pulleys and gears as simple machines, using examples
from everyday life.
      ISBN 1-57572-084-1 (lib. bdg.)
      1. Simple machines- Juvenile literature. 2. Pulleys– Juvenile literature. 3. Gearing – Juvenile
literature. [1. Pulleys. 2. Gearing.]
I. Title. II. Series.
TJ147.G57 1997
621.8' 11—dc20

                                                                    96-15815
                                                                       CIP
                                                                       AC

Acknowledgments
The author and publishers are grateful to the following for permission to reproduce photographs:
The publishers would like to thank the following for permission to reproduce photographs:
Trevor Clifford pp. 4, 5, 12, 14-19, 21, 22, 23; Collections/Keith Pritchard p. 9; Mary Evans Picture
Library p. 10; Skip Novak PPL p. 7; Stockfile/Steven Behr p. 20; TRIP/H Rogers p. 13; Zefa/Damm p. 6.

Cover photograph reproduced with permission of ImageState/ Stephen Jenkins.

The publishers would like to thank Angela Royston for her assistance in the preparation of this edition.

Every effort has been made to contact copyright holders of any material reproduced in this book.
Any omissions will be rectified in subsequent printings if notice is given to the publisher.

The paper used to print this book comes from sustainable sources.

Contents

Some words are shown in bold, **like this**. You can find the definitions for these words in the glossary.

What Are Pulleys and Gears?

Pulleys and gears are special wheels. They help to make some machines move.

When you turn the crank handle on this model windmill, it makes the sails turn. The handle and the sails are linked by a rubber band. This is the **drive belt**. The drive belt is stretched over two pulleys. It makes both pulleys turn together.

drive belt

pulleys

crank handle

The crank handle of this model is linked to the wheels by two gear wheels. The gear wheels have teeth around their edges. Some of the teeth on one wheel fit between some of the teeth on the other wheel. This is called **meshing**.

When one gear wheel turns, its teeth push the teeth on the other gear wheel. This makes the second gear wheel turn as well.

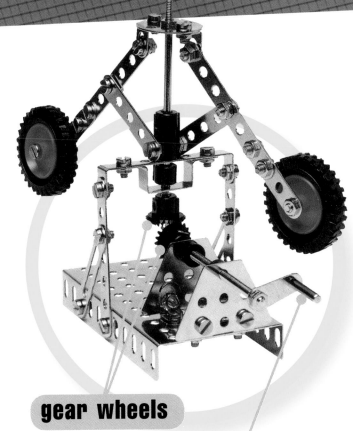

gear wheels

crank handle

FACT FILE Different directions

When two pulleys are linked by a drive belt, they go around in the same direction. Two gear wheels with meshed teeth go around in opposite directions.

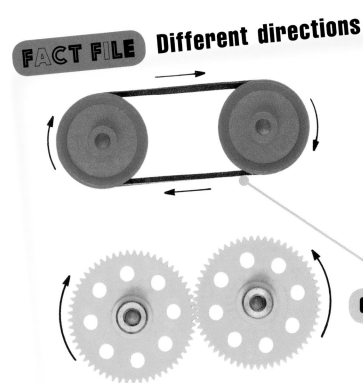

drive belt

Up the Pole

To make a flag go up a pole, you pull down on the rope. As you pull down, the flag goes up. How can a pull down make something go up?

If you look at the top of the pole, you will see the answer. The rope goes over a pulley. The pulley changes the direction of the pull from down to up. So, as you pull down on the rope, the flag goes up.

Can you spot the pulleys on this yacht? Pulleys help sailors to raise the sails up the mast. The sailors pull down on ropes on the deck.

The first pulleys

Who invented the pulley? Nobody knows, but the first pulleys were probably just smooth tree branches. Many people must have had the idea of throwing a rope over a tree branch to lift a heavy load high enough to keep it out of the reach of animals, or to lift it onto a cart.

Cranes and Blocks and Tackles

The hook on this crane is fixed to a pulley. A steel rope runs under the pulley, touching its underside. A powerful **motor** winds the rope up and down to raise the load. Other ropes and pulleys move the load back and forth along the arm of the crane. This arm is called the jib.

jib

steel rope

pulley

load

A block and tackle is a set of pulleys that work together. One person can lift a very heavy weight with a block and tackle. This boat was lifted out of the sea using a block and tackle.

Making it easy

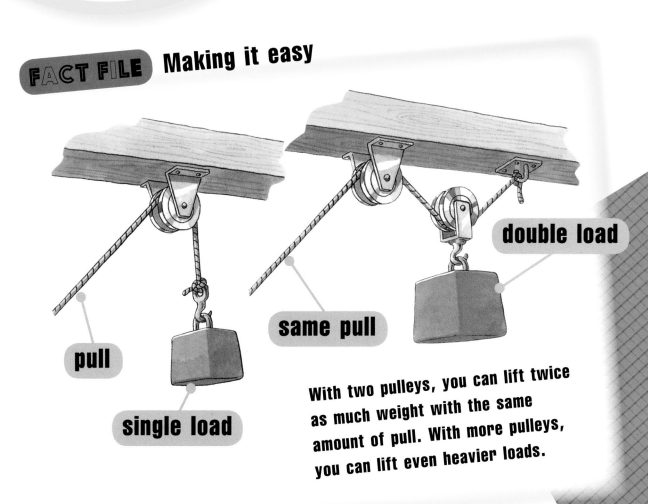

pull

single load

same pull

double load

With two pulleys, you can lift twice as much weight with the same amount of pull. With more pulleys, you can lift even heavier loads.

Drive Belts

A **steam engine** drives this old-fashioned sewing machine. The engine is joined to the sewing machine by pulleys and a **drive belt**. The pulley on the machine is smaller than the pulley on the engine. This makes the sewing machine turn faster than the engine.

These pulley wheels are linked by a drive belt. Two wheels of the same size turn at the same speed.

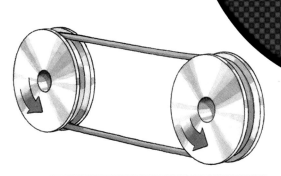

same size, same speed

small pulley　**large pulley**

fast　**slow**

When the wheels are different sizes, the smaller wheel turns faster than the bigger one.

You can make pulley wheels turn in opposite directions by twisting and crossing over the drive belt.

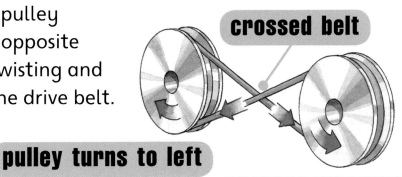

crossed belt

pulley turns to left

pulley turns to right

FACT FILE Half the size, twice the speed

If one pulley is half the size of the other pulley, it turns around twice as quickly. This is because one turn of the large pulley makes the small pulley go around twice.

11

Power Pulleys

Many rides at the amusement park go around and around. Some of them are worked by **steam engines** with pulleys and **drive belts**. This is a model of an old steam engine. It has a drive belt that turns the back wheel to drive the engine along.

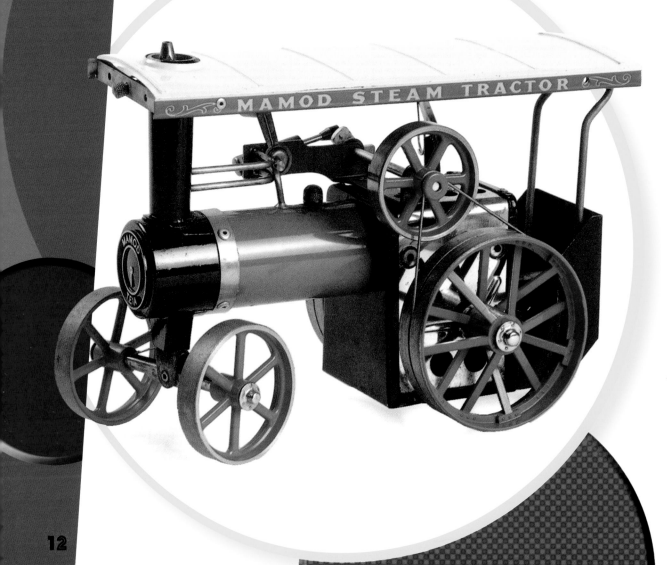

This machine crushes sugarcane to get the juice. It has many moving parts. A steam engine drives it. Drive belts, pulleys, and gears make the parts go around.

Gear Kits

You can learn about gears by making models with a gear kit. Flat, round gears are called **spur gears**. One spur gear can turn several other gears. This is called a **gear train**. The gears in the train go around in different directions. If the gears are different sizes, they go around at different speeds.

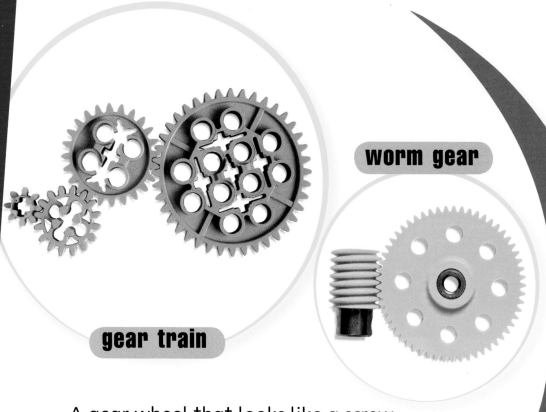

worm gear

gear train

A gear wheel that looks like a screw is called a **worm gear**. When a worm gear turns, it makes a large spur gear go around very slowly.

Two gear wheels can be linked together with a chain that fits over their teeth. This is how the gears on a bicycle work. The chain makes both gear wheels go around in the same direction.

FACT FILE **Count the teeth**

These three gear wheels have seven, ten, and fourteen teeth. Which two gears would you choose to make one gear turn twice as fast as the other? Look at page 24 to see if you were right.

Drills, Whisks, and Reels

When you turn the handle on this drill, it makes the drill bit turn at high speed. The drill bit is held in the **chuck**. The handle is linked to the chuck by bevel gears. Bevel gears have sloping teeth. They change the direction in which things turn.

The gear wheel on the handle is much bigger than the gear wheels on the chuck. This means that the chuck goes around several times each time the handle turns once.

bevel gears

handle

chuck

This hand whisk has two blades. They are turned by gear wheels on either side of the big gear wheel on the handle. The blades turn in opposite directions, so everything mixes in very well.

gears

handle

blades

FACT FILE **Changing direction**

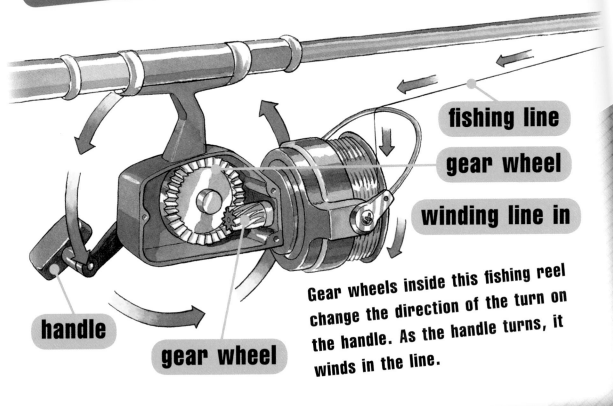

fishing line

gear wheel

winding line in

handle

gear wheel

Gear wheels inside this fishing reel change the direction of the turn on the handle. As the handle turns, it winds in the line.

Clocks and Watches

The three hands on a clock or watch go around at different speeds. The same **mechanism** turns them all. Each hand is linked to the mechanism by different gears.

During the time the hour hand turns one complete circle, the minute hand turns twelve times. Extra gears help the hour hand go more slowly than the minute hand.

hour hand

minute hand

second hand

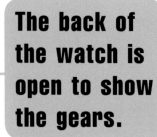

The back of the watch is open to show the gears.

Gears turn the hands of a cuckoo clock. They are powered by falling weights instead of a **motor**. Extra gears turn the parts that make the cuckoo pop out every hour.

Mountain Bikes

The chain on a mountain bike fits over the teeth on special gear wheels. These wheels are called **sprockets**. The chain carries the push on the pedals to the back wheel. This push turns the back wheel.

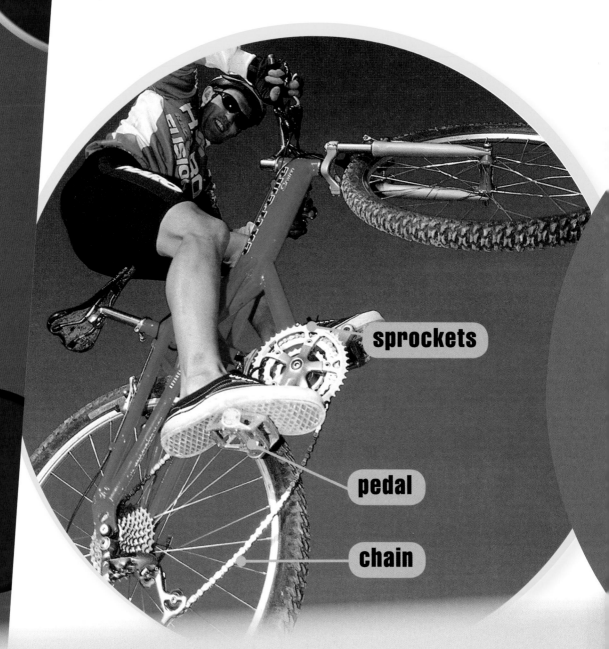

sprockets

pedal

chain

small sprockets

large sprockets

When you change gear on a bike, the chain moves between different sized sprockets on the back wheel. Large sprockets are low gears for climbing hills. Small sprockets are high gears for going fast along flat ground.

FACT FILE How many gears?

Some mountain bikes have 28 gears! Track racing bikes have only one gear.

Activities

A simple pulley

1. Tie a long piece of thread or string to a thick book.
2. Use the string to lift up the book.

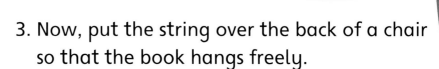

3. Now, put the string over the back of a chair so that the book hangs freely.
4. Pull down on the string to lift up the book.
5. Which way of lifting the book is easier?

See pages 6–7 to find out why.

Gears in action

1. You will need a hand whisk like the one in the photo.
2. Slowly turn the handle and watch what happens.

3. The handle turns the big cog wheel.
4. The big cog wheel turns the two small cog wheels.
5. How many times does each beater go around when you turn the handle once?

See page 11 for an explanation.

Glossary

chuck   part on a drill that grips the different sized drill bits

drive belt   loop of leather or rubber that links one pulley wheel to another

gear train   series of gear wheels that carry turning movements from one part of a machine to another

mechanism   parts that move together to make a machine work

mesh   when the teeth on two gear wheels fit together

motor   machine that uses electricity or fuel (such as gasoline or coal) to make things move

sprocket   toothed wheel on the pedals and back wheel of a bicycle

spur gear   flat, circular gear with teeth around the edge

steam engine   motor or engine that uses steam from boiling water to make things move

worm gear   gear like a screw with a spiral thread running around its surface

Index

The answer to the question on page 15 is:
The seven-toothed wheel goes twice as fast as the fourteen-toothed wheel.